MW01038777

O LUTEFISK
(THE BOOK)

BY
E.C. "RED" STANGLAND

A Nostalgic Look Back To Those Good Old Days

Growing Up
— In A Norwegian-American Family
— In A Small Town
— In The 1920's and 30's

ILLUSTRATED BY MARIAN HENJUM

PUBLISHED BY
NORSE PRESS
P.O. BOX 1554
SIOUX FALLS, S. DAK. 57101
1SBN 0 961 3274-1-3

Other Books By Red Stangland

Norwegian Jokes

Son of Norwegian Jokes

Grandson of Norwegian Jokes

Uff Da Jokes

More Uff Da Jokes

Polish & Other Ethnic Jokes

Office Jokes

Yankee Jokes

(The entire series is published by Norse Press
Box 1554, Sioux Falls, S.D. 57101)

Also:

"How to become your own boss"

A practical guide to attaining self-employment
and earning more money.

You may send to the above address
for more information.

Dedication

To the memory of my sister
Mildred Stangland Baker
1912-1985

And to my other siblings,
Orv, Bill and Gretchen

~ Lutefisk ~

A Gift of Cod that passeth all understanding.

Preface

If a wave of nostalgia grips you when you catch the scent of wood smoke, and if the sound of a steam railroad whistle in an old late-night movie brings waves of deja vu to your consciousness . . . you may be ready for a trip back in time via this collection of vignettes about the 1920's and 30's.

Just as the old hand pump usually needed some priming, so it can be with your memory to be programmed to pour forth details of what the times and life were like when you were young, or when your parents or grandparents were, depending on your current age.

Such drastic changes have taken place since the 30's that it seems like an entirely different world today compared to the lifestyles of a generation or two ago.

If you are from the current generation, you can learn about conditions your parents endured as well as the good times that people had when things were much simpler than they are today.

CONTENTS

O LUTEFISK

In 1978, I wrote the words to a poem and titled it O LUTEFISK. It was written to go along with the tune of O Tannenbaum. As I put the four stanzas together, a multitude of childhood memories came to mind, including thoughts of my very Norwegian family. My mother and dad were both brought up in Norway. Dad came over in 1882 with his first wife and her parents, the Ostroots. When his first wife died in 1904, Dad went back to Norway to find a Norwegian bride. He met a young lady, 24 years his junior, who had a dressmaking shop combined with a small convenience store in Stavanger. (Forerunner of the 7-Eleven stores?) This 28 year old seamstress came to the United States in 1906 at which time they got married and brought five children into the world. I was the youngest and I'm actually surprised to be here since my dad was 68 years old when I was born! If he were alive today, he would be 131; so you could say that I came from a real OLD Norwegian background. All of my ancestors as far as I can trace were from Norway . . . except for some Swedes that I found in the family tree from back in the 1300's.

So, as I sat down to write a poem for a song about lutefisk, I let my mind wander to the days when Mom and Dad were alive and in good health, and lutefisk was their special treat. (Not necessarily appreciated 100% by their Americanized offspring.)

One of the humorous memories of Mom and her lutefisk occurred back in the '40s. Mom was keeping her latest supply of lutefisk in a scrub pail which she placed outside the back door to keep cool (it was December). When it was discovered that the lutefisk had disappeared, we finally concluded that the garbage man had spotted the Norwegian delicacy and decided it was to be put aboard his truck as a pail of garbage.

Mom never quite got over the shock, especially since the rest of us found it so funny. Mom didn't see anything funny about it at all. To her, it was definitely an UFF DA!

"O LUTEFISK"

O Lutefisk. . .O Lutefisk. . .how fragrant your aroma
O Lutefisk. . .O Lutefisk. . .You put me in a coma.
You smell so strong. . .you look like glue
You taste yust like an overshoe
But Lutefisk. . .come Saturday
I tink I'll eat you anyvay.

O Lutefisk. . .O Lutefisk. . .I put you by the doorvay
I vanted you to ripen up. . .yust like dey do in Norvay
A dog came by and sprinkled you. . .I hit him
    vid an army shoe
O Lutefisk. . .now I suppose
I'll eat you as I hold my nose.

O Lutefisk. . .O Lutefisk. . .how vell I do remember
On Christmas eve how we'd receive. . .our big
    treat of December
It vasn't turkey or fried ham. . .it vasn't even
    pickled spam
My mudder knew dere vas no risk. . .
In serving buttered lutefisk.

O Lutefisk. . .O Lutefisk. . .now everyone discovers
Dat Luefisk and lefse makes. . .Norvegians better lovers
Now all da vorld can have a ball. . .you're better
    dan dat Yeritol
O Lutefisk. . .vid brennevin
You make me feel like Errol Flynn.

-E.C. STANGLAND

GROWING UP "NORWEGIAN"

When you have parents who were both born in Norway, you assume a certain point of view that is somehow different from the rest of your companions. My parents. . . Mother particularly, drummed into us the unquestioned superiority of being Norwegian. At one time, I was even convinced God was Norwegian, which naturally made Jesus a Norwegian too. As a consequence, it came as a surprise when it dawned on me that not everyone in our town was Norwegian. There were even a few "Blue belly Yankees" in our midst. It really wasn't talked about a great deal until May 17th when the annual Syttende Mai fever settled on our community. This was the day of great celebration, with a brief parade in our two block downtown district.

A makeshift Viking ship carried Charlie Starksen, the local general store owner, and Mrs. Sam Vedvei, the entire float being mounted on a dray wagon and pulled by a team of horses. Immediately following this impressive procession, the great ball game of the year took place: The Norwegians vs. The Skunks, engaged in a fierce battle of softball (called kittenball in those days). After nine innings of good natured jibes between the Norwegians and the Unbelievers, the Norwegian identity was put away for another year and we all became Americans again. Except, of course, for my mother. She taught us the Norwegian table prayer which we were required to recite at every meal. It was in Norwegian, but it wasn't until I was an adult that I understood what the words meant.

I Jesu Navn
gaar vi til Bords
at spise og drikke
paa dit Ord;
dig Gud til Are
os til Gavn,
saa faar vi Mat
i Jesu Navn,
Amen.

In Jesus' name we go to the table
To eat and drink at your word
To God the honor and us the gain
So shall we eat in Jesus' name.

UNDERSTATED NORWEGIANISMS

Norwegian-Americans have a distinctive way of expressing themselves...especially in communities where they have retained a lot of old-country ways. This was brought home to me last year when I was getting ready to leave Norway by plane after a two week visit. On the shuttle to the airport, I started visiting with my seat mate, a gentleman who turned out to be from my city. His name was Norman Eitrheim, he said, but I couldn't place him. Finally, I asked if he was connected with the Valley National Bank.

"No," he answered modestly. "I'm the Bishop of the American Lutheran Church for South Dakota."

After I regained my composure, we chatted about his hometown of Baltic, S.D., which is sometimes referred to as "Little Norway." In Baltic, even grandchildren of Norwegian immigrants sometimes retain the Norwegian brogue, such as pronouncing their "z" sounds as "esses." President, thus, becomes "Pressident."

Anyway, Norman (the Bishop, that is) reflected on the quaint way that Norwegians conversed in Baltic, such as when two farmers meet in town on Saturday night. Ole, dressed in clean overalls, a wool plaid shirt and flowered tie under the overall bib, would encounter Lars on the corner with a quizzical remark, "Yah, so you're in town too?" "Yah," Lars would respond. "I guess so."

This tentative answer is typical of many Norwegian-Americans. Many times their statements are in the form of a question, such as "I vonder if it might be raining," or "I vonder if it isn't hot today," instead of "It's raining out," or "It sure is hot." An understatement is more the Norwegian way.

Even Norwegian insults are expressed in a distinctive way. . . using infinitives to describe the subject. So, instead of saying, "Olav drinks like a fish," the Norwegian will say, "Yah, dat Olav. . he's so terrible to drink." Or, "Yah, Lena. . . she's so terrible to eat."

Even compliments are expressed in this manner, to wit:

"Dagny is so good to play the flute," (instead of Dagny is a fine musician).

Bishop Eitrheim chuckled as he recalled other Norwegian modes of expression.

Phone rings: "Hello. . . is dat you, Trygve?"

"Yah, I tink so."

Sometimes, says Norman, the Norwegian pronunciations can be confusing. One minute the farmer is commenting, "I better cut da oats. . . dey're getting jellow." A half hour later, he's at the dining room table saying, "Vould you pass da Yello?"

The Bishop wound up our conversation by commenting on how Norwegians often fill in a lull in the conversation with a short inward breath, enunciating the word "Yah." I noticed that among my relatives in Norway, too.

I wonder. . . can that be a Norwegian characteristic?

That Norman Eitrheim, he's so good to remember how Norwegians talk.

American Norwegianisms:

"Did you see a fox around here today?"
"No, but I saw vun day before yesterday night."

"Where is da Gunderson place?"
"Oh. . . it's about a mile north and a half."

A TRIBUTE TO NORWEGIAN PARENTS

When I was but a youngster, I often wondered why
My parents spoke with accents unlike the folks near by
Instead of saying Johnson, as spoken with a "J"
They'd pronounce it "Yohnson" as "J" became a "Yay".

My folks were born in Norway, along the scenic fjords
And they came to this country for what this land affords
To claim the rich potential of America's proud dream
The ownership of property. . . that immigrants esteem

My Dad worked as a farmer on fertile midwest soil
With teams of mules and horses and honest Nordic toil
His own farm, home and children. . . came to him by and
     by
Still, memories of Norway would linger in his eye.

My mother dreamed of Norway and of her family there
While raising up her children with tender love and care
We all remember lefse, and Jule brod so good
All made upon a cookstove that we had fed with wood

Those grand old folks are gone now. . . but I remember yet
The fine Norwegian heritage that I cannot forget
Of working hard and honestly, the qualities that stay
The simple things brought with them. . . from their own
     land, Norway.

They never had much money. . . or property to leave
They left me only memories of childhood to retrieve
But what they left is priceless, a gift of which I'm proud
It was their Norwegian heritage that Mom and Dad
     endowed.

                    -E.C. STANGLAND

ARE YOU AN OLD TIMER?

Most of us who have been around for five or six decades have some memories that the younger generation doesn't share. So, we can safely say that you are an old timer if you can remember: when men wore flat straw hats in the summer and women wore "cloche" or bell shaped hats somewhat resembling Tupperware bowls; when Nehi was one of the more popular soda pop beverages (and local comics would pose this question: Nehi for a nickel; how far for a dime?) When you had to crank a car to get it started; when you customarily expected to patch a tire on any long trip; when bus tokens were 3 for a quarter in the cities; when there were mainly gravel and dirt roads to get around on; when expressions like: "23 Skidoo," and "so's your old man" were frequently used; when Montgomery Ward catalogues were used in lieu of toilet paper; when air was clean and sex was dirty; when cars had running boards; when Fox Movietone and other newsreels preceded every movie you went to; when there were no Technicolor movies; when there was no sales tax; when there were no touchtone OR dial telephones...just "Central;" when paper boys went up and down the street yelling—"EXTRA, EXTRA, READ ALL ABOUT IT!" When Dillinger and his gang roamed the country holding up banks; when daredevil aviators did stunt flying shows in your town; when farmers could get by with a team of horses and a plow; when cars used inner-tubes; when there were only dinky tourist cabins for travelers to stay in or a regular hotel; when "Boarding Houses" were common for single people to be fed at; when every town, large or small, had a dance hall; when there were no super-markets; when every town had a blacksmith shop and still shoed horses; when many townspeople's garages were converted stables. If many, or most of these are among your memories, then you qualify as a genuine OLD TIMER!

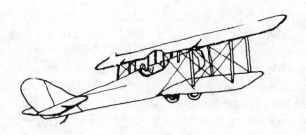

FIRSTS

Indelible in a person's memory is the FIRST time a certain sight is experienced. There were several firsts I can still recall. When I saw my first airplane in the sky, I watched in open mouthed wonder. I ran a mile south of town when I saw it had begun landing. Breathless, I watched the machine taxi across a farm pasture. Thereupon, the pilot came out of a cockpit and talked to some locals about going up in the air for a dollar. I was transfixed as I watched a farmer climb into the machine and the pilot gunned the motor, taking off across the pasture until the plane leaped into the sky.

My first view of American Indians occured in our town one summer day. I don't recall the occasion, but this group of Indians put on a short pow wow on our main street. They didn't seem to be of this world. Their costumes, hair styles and beadwork, along with their Indian chanting and peculiar dance, were enough to make a goggle-eyed youngster stand and stare in awe.

A similar reaction occurred when I saw a black person for the first time. The neighboring town of Lake Preston had a Watermelon Day festivity every Labor Day. . .with free watermelon for everyone. Also, a carnival was in town and hundreds, if not thousands, of people were on hand. There in Lake preston, while feasting on free watermelon, I saw a Negro for the first time. It is currently unfashionable to associate watermelon with blacks, but this black man, the first I had seen, was enjoying the delicacy with no less enthusiasm than any of the Norwegians who had come to town for this annual free treat.

Another "first" that shocked us kids . . . was the day one of our pack came running, yelling, "Hey . . . there's a woman smoking at Skip's Restaurant." This we had to see! A woman SMOKING! We soon verified it, four little twerps, standing outside the cafe staring in at a woman ACTUALLY puffing away at a cigarette! We couldn't have been more astounded by a two-headed boy or a calf with 7 legs. For days we talked to the other kids who hadn't witnessed the spectacle.

Another rare sight in Hetland were the gypsy caravans that paid the town a visit from time to time. When they came to town, I went into hiding because it was a well-known "fact" that gypsies kidnapped children. They came into town in big black cars. Their rather luxurious mode of transportation was a sharp contract to the strange clothing they wore and the apparent lack of regular employment. As a kid, I couldn't understand what they wanted . . . whether it was begging, or what. But apparently they had some method of commerce, such as reading fortunes, selling trinkets, or maybe swapping with local denizens. After an hour or so around town, the entire menage would pile back into their bag cars and disappear out of town.

DO YOU REMEMBER?

How long has it been since you saw an old fashioned General Store with a ladder that rolled along a track above, allowing the clerk to climb to reach a row of shoes stacked above the normal reach? The little General Stores of my childhood were like that. They not only sold groceries, but you could also order men's clothing, ladies ready-to-wear and children's togs. The general store in my town also served as the post office.

All coffee sold was ground on the premises, which is why the store always smelled pleasantly of freshly ground coffee. This was as close as you got to "instant coffee."

Another feature of the small grocery in the old days was that often the grocery clerks would put up an order for the customer. I recall my Mother would call the Council Oak Grocery with her list. The clerks eventually learned to understand Mom's Norwegian-accented English, so we generally got all of the items Mother had ordered. But, sometimes a new clerk would mess up because Mom would pronounce 8 as "ight" and we would occasionally come up with five items instead.

Some of the larger dry goods stores had a novel system of conveying cash to the store office up on the balcony. They had a system where cash was put in a cup affair which then screwed into a sort of trolley system from the ground floor to the upper cash office. The clerk would then pull a handle and the cup would go flying up the trolley wire until it reached the cashiers hands. With this system, one cashier could handle several departments in the store. Some of the swankier stores had pneumatic tubes to convey the money, much like those used by drive-in banks today.

CHARLIE'S GENERAL STORE

Among the things I miss the most (it nearly brings on tears)
Is the old-time General store I knew. . . back in my younger
    years.
No fancy super markets then. . . no plastic blister packs
Just plain old-fashioned merchandise, lined up in rows and
    stacks.

In my old home town we had. . . just one small general store
It seemed to serve our every need. . . we seldom wanted
    more.
Mama bought her yard goods there. . . as well as hats and
    shoes
And all the town folk gathered there to hear the latest news.

I still recall the pleasant smell of coffee freshly ground
And pickles soaked in brine dispensed from barrels big and
    round.
Smoked herring was a special treat, displayed in open air
We even got our school supplies and Long John underwear.

Old Charlie was a dapper man with pin stripe suit and tie
He'd sit there at his roll top desk while customers walked by.
He knew far more than banker Jones. . . the finances in the
    town
And when some folks were short on cash, Old Charlie'd "jot
    it down."

Penny candy was a treat. . . it seemed I looked for hours
While Mama bought her garden seeds for vegetables and
  flowers.
The Sunday roast we sometimes had. . . came from the old
  meat case
No frozen meats or other foods that lack that old time taste.

Charlie's store is gone now. . . and Charlie is laid to rest
But I sure miss the sights and smells that had the old time
  zest.
I'd love to go there every week. . . and then come back for
  more
For, there'll never be another spot. . . like Charlie's General
  Store.

-E.C. STANGLAND

EXTENDED FAMILY

Growing up in a small town meant that you were part of an extended family. That is, everyone kept an eye on each other in a benevolent manner. We kids were allowed a great deal of freedom around the village. That meant we had the run of the depot, the lumber yard, the hardware store warehouse, the grain elevators, etc. In fact, we more or less regarded everything in town "community property." If we wanted to play ball, any vacant lot in town was fair game. Our little world was our playground and the entire adult population saw to it that we didn't get out of line. We were tolerantly regarded as harmless kids by most of the town. The exceptions were the grouches who did not subscribe to the unwritten custom of putting up with kids and their unlimited energy. The occasional grumps, however, were not suffered in silence...we kids could dream up all sorts of torment by teasing, taunting and sometimes playing tricks...such a tipping over outhouses on Halloween or verbally hooting at the individual as they ambled about the village. We were sassy at times, but never outright mean or destructive. Somehow, violence was not part of our society at that time.

These were gentler times and even in adversity, most people would not resort to thievery or acts of violence. Somehow, I feel those times had a special atmosphere that we could use in the 1980's. This is not to say there were not acts of mischief, such as when a local outhouse was removed from its location and rolled on logs to the railroad where a bunch of older boys heisted it onto a flat car. It ended up in Illinois and it was a couple of months before it finally returned to its rightful owner.

Then, there was the incident where a buggy was fastened to the flagpole rope in the center of our two-block downtown and hoisted to the top. My brother Wilbur tells about the school's principal and his lecture about doing good for poor people on Halloween and how, on Halloween night, in his boyhood he and his companions would chop wood for the less fortunate. My brother and his peers took the sermon to heart and thus when the Principal came out his back door the following morning, there was his outhouse, tipped over with a note attached: "Here's your wood. Now, chop it!"

"I'M GLAD TO BE A NORWEGIAN"

When you mention nationality and think of "what you are"
It often brings up references to foreign lands afar
Of course, we know "American" is our nationality
But all of us have ethnic roots that denote our family tree

For my part, I claim Norwegian as my ancestral tie
And I believe that Viking look still lingers in my eye
A thousand years ago, they say, the Vikings ruled the seas
And conquered many kingdoms in long boats
   made from trees

Leif Erickson went sailing with Vikings ships and crew
And they discovered Vinland around one thousand two
The land's now called America. . . history tells us that,
Discovered by a Norseman back when the world was "flat."

Rocky Norway's climate and meager farming land
Made our ancestors emigrate, as we can understand
And so here in America we have so many "sons"
Like Olson, Nelson, Hanson, and Johnsons by the tons.

We have Gunsmoke's own Matt Dillon, who's a
   Norwegian boy;
Knute Rockne and Sonja Henie were America's
   pride and joy.
Many thousand others have brought their Nordic skill
And made us proud of heritage that lingers with us still.

It's OK to be German, or Pole or Dane or Swede
And even being English would make me proud indeed
But somehow there's a special feeling that fills me
  deep inside
And that is being NORWEGIAN, for it is my ethnic pride.

So all you sons of Norway, and all you daughters too
Remember Norwegian heritage and what it means to you.
With Lutefisk and lefse and other Norsky food
We keep that special feeling, that real Norwegian mood.

I'm glad to be Norwegian and all that it implies
Of honest working people with good, strong family ties
We love our land, America, in everything we do
And glad are we to say, that we do love Norway too.

-E.C. STANGLAND

THE VAPO RUB CURE

During my childhood, I can't remember any medication other than Vapo Rub. I never went to the doctor nor did the doctor ever come to see me . . . that is, after I was born (at home, by the way). So, whatever childhood diseases I had, my mother must have taken care of all of them with simple home remedies, plenty of tender loving care, and hot plates. I can still remember cuddling up to a dinner plate warmed up in my mother's cook stove oven. It seemed to alleviate whatever ache or malfunction that prevailed. Leg aches, chill blains, stomach ache, colds, whatever it was, the warm plate and Vapo Rub was the only treatment I knew. I still am not much for medications and I rarely have any serious ailment. But when I do, I use a hot pad (electric) to take my mind off the discomfort, and a moderate application of Vapo Rub. Mama's prescription still works best.

RUB A DUB DUB

You can't really say you have lived through the 20's and 30's if you have never bathed in a galvanized wash tub. Probably nothing in the household in the old days got a heavier workout than that old metal tub that served as our bath tub and then did double duty as a laundry tub. Every so often. . .when my mother could catch me. . .I had to have my bath in that old tub. Mom would heat water in a kettle on the old cook stove and off would come layers of grime I had accumulated by playing in the dirt and rooting around like a gopher. I usually had enough dirt washed off of me to start a small garden after the water was poured out. The soap Mom used was certainly not Dove or Caress. . .more than likely it was a bar of Fels Naphtha or that awful soap that smelled like Lysol, Lifebuoy. (Joke from the old days: "Let me hold your Palm Olive." "Not on your Life, Boy!")

Red Foley once made a recording in which he said, "I'd almost rather eat a bug. . .than take a bath in that old galvanized washing tub."

Amen!

FARMERS' SATURDAY NIGHT

Saturday was a big day in our little town . . . the day the farmers would bring in their crates of eggs and cans of cream. The stores would do their best business all week on that one day. And Saturday night was the busiest time because the farmers would have finished their chores and were ready for a little relaxation. While the Mrs. was doing the grocery shopping, the farmer would stand around on Main street, leaning on his car or sitting on the fender while the townspeople and other farmers would exchange bits of gossip. It was considered a mark of prestige to be in town first so you could park right in front of the grocery store. Any farmer who could accomplish that feat would be considered more prosperous, perhaps, because maybe he had a hired man to do the chores while he went to town early. Or, maybe it merely marked him as more efficient and capable.

The farmers' Saturday night uniform invariably was a combination of a pair of clean overalls and a second-best suit coat. (The best suit was saved for church and funerals.) The more fastidiously dressed farmers sported either a work shirt or a dress shirt with a big flowered tie tucked into the bib of their overalls.

BARNYARD INSULATION

During the 20s and 30s, I don't think anyone had heard about commercial insulation, like the fiberglass batts we have in our attic. (Speaking of attics, I haven't seen old fashioned attic like we had in the old days for at least 35 years, where you could find old furniture and pictures of ancestors).

But, getting back to insulation, the standard method used by many householders in the old days was to pile straw and manure around the base of the house and leave it there all winter. It apparently had some insulation value and no doubt cut down on coal bills for the winter. Another fuel saving measure was the flexiglass-type material nailed over the storm windows for the winter. Since double paned windows and other advances in the storm window business, I haven't seen straw and manure piled around a house in years. Matter of fact, the old fashioned storm windows have given way to self storing non-rusting steel units that can be converted in a jiffy to screened windows. I can remember to this day climbing a ladder every spring and fall to wrestle with those heavy pesky storm windows and clumsy screens. Now, that's one convenience I won't argue with. . . nostalgia or not.

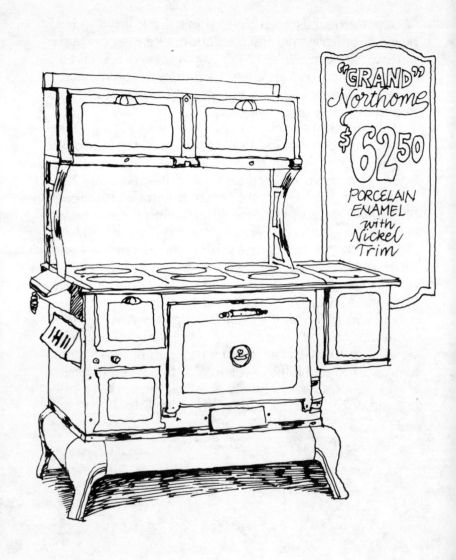

"GRAND"
Northome
$62.50
PORCELAIN
ENAMEL
with
Nickel
Trim

"MAMA'S OLD COOK STOVE"

If I live to be a hundred. . . I never will forget
The days when Mama used to feed. . . a most
    unusual "pet"
Her pride and joy for many years. . . became her treasure
    trove
It was the family centerpiece. . . t'was Mama's
    old cook stove.

A cob she dipped in kerosene. . . served to light the fire
Sometimes lumps of coal would make. . . the temperature
    go higher
But generally the fuel she used. . . to fire the stove up good
Was splintered on the chopping stump. . .just plain old
    kindling wood.

Now, Mama was a wizard. . . at baking cakes and pies
And I loved to watch the biscuit dough as it would
    slowly rise
The homemade bread that we enjoyed. . . will ne'er
    be duplicated
Upon the modern kitchen range that looks so complicated.

The old cook stove did not have dials. . . or thermostats
    and such
But Mama knew the formula to make it do so much.
It fried the meat and cooked the soup. . .
    for every meal it toiled
And Mama's great egg coffee would warble as it boiled.

No microwave could do as well. . . as Mama's
    ancient range
When modern stoves came on the scene, she didn't
    want to change.
Why, it even heated water in the crusted reservoir
We used it for the dishes, and for scrubbing up the floor.

The friendly oven warmed us up when chilled by
   snow and rain
It heated flat-irons and dinner plates when anyone
   had pain
Sis came down with pneumonia. . . and the only cure
   Mom knew
Was to keep her warm with platters that the stove
   had heated through.

Quite often Mom made lefse. . . upon the large stove top
But first she'd shine it up with wax. . . from bread
   wrappers wadded up
Flour and potatoes would be mixed as she hummed a
   Norwegian song
We'd sniff the air expectantly. . . we knew it wouldn't
   be long.

Although my Mama's gone now. . . and the stove has
   turned to rust
I still recall the bygone days. . . and the kitchen range
   we'd trust
To fix our food and cure our ills. . . it served us
   many ways.
And the memory of Mom's old cook stove. . . recalls
   those bygone days.

Mama's old black cooking stove. . . with shiny metal trim
We kept it full with cobs and wood. . . and coal up to
   the brim
I long for carefree days gone by. . . as I let my
   memories rove
And I recall those good things made. . . on Mama's
   old cook stove.

                              -E.C. STANGLAND

THE MEDICINE SHOW

Live entertainment was scarce in our small town. When I was four, the Medicine Show came to town. Oh, what excitement! It featured a dramatic play, UNCLE TOM'S CABIN. One night was amateur night and my big sister, Milly, pressured me to learn a song about a "little boy and a little girl," the story being that the girl said she would allow the boy "just one kiss. . . when the apples grow upon the lilac tree." The clever little boy, so the song told, was seen the next morning tying apples on the lilac tree. My soulful rendition won first prize, based no doubt on my precocity; and the $2 that I won was swiftly invested (after careful study of the Montgomery Ward catalogue) in a pair of boots with a pocket knife.

In between features, patent medicine was sold to the crowd, plus boxes of candy with "valuable prizes" inside.

Mama got into the act when the Medicine Show man offered a greased pig free to any woman who could come to the stage and hold onto it. Mama, having been a farm wife, went right up and knew just how to grab the pig and hold it without it getting away. We kept the pig in our shed where Mama fattened it on table scraps and corn. When it got to butchering size, a farmer friend butchered it and kept us in good food all winter long. Besides, Mama used the tallow to make soap, and the head was used for head cheese. Nothing went to waste!

WHAT HAPPENED TO THE SAWDUST?

It has been a long time since I was in an honest to goodness old fashioned butcher shop with sawdust on the floor. These days, the meat is pre-packaged, immaculately wrapped in plastic, pre-priced and extremely impersonal. Chances are you not only don't talk to the butcher, you don't even SEE him. But the old time butchers were constantly on stage. . .wrestling with quarters of beef, trimming a roast, putting up an order of wieners (real ones, linked together in real casings), or grinding a tub full of hamburger. And all the while smilingly serving his patrons, and sometimes even collecting for the purchase. The butcher gave genuine personal service. . .I really miss the contact, the conversation. And as a kid, many was the time the butcher would hand me a free weiner!

Won't someone be innovative and bring back an old fashioned-type butcher shop, cut his own beef and pork, sprinkle fresh sawdust on the floor, and wait on customers one at a time? But it has to smell like, and have the feel of the old fashioned meat market. . . with sawdust on the floor. I won't even object if I catch him weighing his thumb.

WHEN MEN WERE MEN...
AND HAIR WAS GREASY

Do you remember...slicked down hair? We never heard of the "dry look" because oily hair was the only way to keep that mop of hair laying down. So, bottles of Brilliantine hair tonic and other gooey concoctions were a regular part of every man's grooming. No self respecting male would have ever dreamed of having a permanent such as you sometimes see worn today.

Do you remember when shave and a haircut, four bits, was a regular regimen of American males? The barber would use a straight edge razor and would sharpen the blade frequently on a leather strap, hanging from the barber chair. This was before Norelcos, Remingtons, and the safety razors with disposable blades. Speaking of shaving...do you remember the Burma Shave signs along the roads? This was before cars started traveling at near supersonic speeds, so a road sign was not only easy to read, but also helped to prevent boredom during a slow ride. Burma Shave had a series of signs placed in a row.

For example:

SHAVING BRUSH
DON'T YOU CRY
YOU'LL BE A SHOE DAUBER
BY AND BY
BURMA SHAVE

It was a very effective means of advertising and made the Burma Shave people a mint.

MY GET UP AND GO
has got up and went

How do I know that my youth is all spent?
My "get up and go" has got up and went.
Still, I don't mind when I think with a grin
Of all the grand places my "get up" has been.

Old age is golden, so I've heard it said.
But, sometimes I wonder as I get into bed.
With my ears in the drawer and my teeth in a cup,
My eyes on the table until I wake up.

As sleep fills my eyes, I say to myself,
"Is there anything else I can put on the shelf?"
I think to myself as I close the door,
"My friends are the same. . .perhaps even more."

When I was young, my slippers were red
I could kick up my heels right over my head
And then I grew older. . .my slippers were blue
Still I could dance the glorious night through.

Now that I'm old, my slippers are black
I walk to the store and puff all the way back.
How do I know that my youth is all spent?
Well, my "get up and go" has got up and went.

Now that I've retired from life's competition
I somehow have lost my old-time ambition
My medicine chest is filled to the brim
And I'm living on pills to keep me in trim.

I get up each morning and dust off my wits
I pick up the paper and I read the obits
If my name is still missing, I know I'm not dead
So, I eat a good breakfast and I go back to bed!"

DRUG STORES

If there is one institution that existed in the "good old days" that would be heaven to bring back to the modern day, it would be the old fashioned drug store. What could be closer to paradise to a youngster than a drug store in those days. . . candy galore, ice cream treats and soda fountain delights, plus toys on display at Christmas time. All the sights and smells of things desirable to mankind must have been created for the town drug store.

How many times did I stand before the candy counter with a nickel gripped tightly in my fingers, trying to come to a decision on just what combination I could buy for that great big nickel. A licorice stick, that was a penny. Some candies were 5 for a penny, so there was usually an assortment of gumdrops, chocolate covered peanuts, jawbreakers, etc. After the momentous decision had been made, the druggist would patiently put my selection in a paper sack and off I'd go with one of my buddies to enjoy the sugar banquet. Good grief. . . no wonder my teeth were almost ruined by the time I was 13 years old!

The most memorable thing about the old drug store was the distinctive odor of chemicals. It is hard to describe. . . but there were certain substances the druggist kept on hand that gave every drug store in the land the same sort of smell. It wasn't perfumy. . . . just a different kind of odor that you never experience in the modern drug store. You could walk into such a store with your eyes closed and know immediately where you were.

And the soda fountain? Marble top soda fountain of my memories...with the fizz water spigots, the syrups for the ice cream sodas and sundae flavorings. The acetic acid bottle to add a tart taste to the lemon sodas. The large drums of ice cream in the big blocky ice cream freezer.

The drug store always had gallons and gallons of multi flavored ice cream on hand, and a generous size dipper that gave you two scooops for a nickel (or was it a dime?). And the sundaes, topped with fresh roasted nuts, were like paradise in a dish.

Somehow...please, bring back an old fashioned drug store! I will bring you all my business...toothpaste...Kleenex, combs...prescriptions and especially, I will live at the soda fountain. Must be a marble top. Must have ice cream tables and ice cream chairs with twisted metal construction. Must have an old fashioned counter. And above all, it MUST SMELL like the old fashioned drug store.

THE CHOO CHOO

I really miss the steam locomotives that used to go past my house every day. The deep throated steam whistle would announce the train's impending arrival many minutes before the puffing giant came rolling into the station. The Chicago & Northwestern stopped at our little town twice a day on its run between Chicago and Rapid City, S.D. The usual routine would be unloading the mail sacks and any passengers due to debark, or entrain, plus a little conversation between the conductor and the depot agent. I loved the smell of the sulphur scented steam, a product of burning coal that I have not experienced since childhood. How I would love to catch a whiff of that railroad steam once again. (Maybe someone could get rich by producing that essence in an aerosol can and sell it to old timers like me.)

Since the railroad ran right through the center of our town, the depot and the tracks were our playground. We would flatten pennies on the track as well as other objects like washers and nails. And some kids even claimed they could hear when the train left Arlington 5 miles away by putting their ear on the rail.

Our swimming hole was right beside the tracks out east of town and the engineer would often give us a squirt of steam playfully as his iron horse rolled by...probably because we wore no swim suits and the steam was inclined to make us scatter au naturel.

I'll probably never hear that lonesome train whistle again, but I'll never forget it either.

BONFIRES AND BAKED POTATOES

I don't think a baked potato from a fancy restaurant ever tasted half as good as bonfire-baked potatoes from a burning pile of leaves. Our childhood bonfires were spontaneous affairs, usually resulting from having raked the leaves out toward the street. As kids, we would wrestle in the leaves just for the sport and exercise of it, and then as night fell there in the October early chill, a harvest moon would loom overhead and we could almost see witches on broomsticks flying past the luminous disk in the sky. Then came the magic time for the bonfire. . . pungently perfumed dried leaves sending up aromatic clouds of smoke. This, of course, was before we became so aware of air pollution. Leaf burning not only was a ritual, but was considered a right (as well as a rite). Part of the ritual was to bury a few potatoes in the leaves before ignition. When the leaves had succumbed to the flames and glowed as embers, we would poke into the fire with a stick and bring out our roasted potatoes. Steamy and mouth-watering. . . there was no finer treat. How long has it been since YOU had a bonfire-roasted potato? Or, for that matter, smelled and experienced an old fashioned bonfire? Can you remember the last time someone used the expression "bonfire?" I can't.

THE SPINNER

A simple home made toy — the spinning button on a string — could amuse a kid for hours in the 20's and 30's. (Try it yourself, it's still lots of fun.)

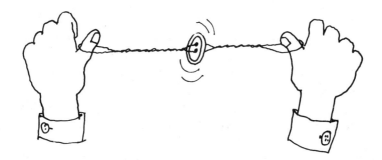

A ten year old kid like me could have a good time with his spinner at school — especially when it spun into the hair of the girl sitting in the desk in front of you and got tangled into her locks.

COULD YOU RUN A COAL FURNACE?

Boy, are we spoiled! Ask the average householder how to regulate a coal furnace, and you will get a blank stare in return. Frankly, I don't recall exactly how it was done. But, a search of my memory tells me that there was a control upstairs consisting of a metal turning device which would transmit by way of a chain into the basement the control to give the coal furnace either more or less air.

"Draft" setting gave more air and increased the heat.

"Check" setting would reduce the air intake and thereby lower the temperature. At night, as I recall, the fire would be banked and the dial put on "check". That would keep things on a controlled level during the night; then, when the first person got up in the morning, the dial could be turned to "draft" and the fire in the furnace would quickly elevate so everyone could get dressed comfortably and come to breakfast. What a contrast with the simple act of using a slight pressure of the forefinger to set the themostat nowadays. Yes, I'm afraid we ARE spoiled today. . . and thankfully so.

(Besides, the nuisance and mess involved in shoveling coal is not missed one iota. Nor is the messy chore of hauling and disposal of ashes and clinkers.)

HOW TO PREPARE LUTEFISK

1. Get some lutefisk
2. Get a piece of pine board
3. Lay lutefisk on the board
4. Flatten lutefisk with a cleaver
5. Sprinkle with pepper and salt
6. Pour on melted butter
7. Heat in stove for two hours
8. Allow to cool down a bit
9. Put on table
10. Throw away lutefisk
11. Eat the board

MAMA'S FIRST BASKETBALL GAME

My brother, Wilbur, was the family athlete. With his 6 foot 2 height, he became a basketball whiz and helped the Hetland team win many victories. Somehow, Mama had never watched him play basketball; and so in his senior year, it was arranged that Mama would get a chance to be a spectator at a game in neighboring Arlington. The Lutheran pastor was kind enough to accompany her to the game and hopefully explain to her some of the intricacies of the sport. As the players came running out onto the court, throwing practice baskets and warming up as they do, Mama was trying to figure out what the game was all about.

As she eyed all of the activity of the warm up skirmishes, she turned to the Pastor with a puzzled query, "Who's vinning now?" (This became a family saying down through the years from Mama's first and only basketball game: "Who's vinning now?").

GRAIN SCAVENGING

One day, my buddies and I determined there was valuable grain lying on the floor of every grain car that was parked on the side track in our town. So, we got our mothers' brooms and commenced to scavenge each random grain of oats until we got together enough to put in a sack, about a bushel. With this giant yield, we dragged the sack to Jerry Bunday's elevator and told him we had grain to sell. I believe we got a dime for it, which was great because it was a profitable result of our free enterprise. Chances are there were splinters in the grain and chances are Jerry sold it for chicken feed. Who knows? But in retrospect, it showed the kindness of the man to little boys that you seldom see anymore.

THE FARM SCENE

Staying on a farm for a kid of 10 or 11 was usually a barrel of fun. So many things to do every day. Using the water tank for a swimming pool was always loads of fun. Playing tag or hide and go seek in the hay mow or jumping from the rafters into the haystack in the barn was also a source of good times. It was really considered daring to climb up to the peak of the barn roof, to the metal cupola where the pigeons congregated. At one time, I caught about a half dozen and took them back to town to keep as pets in a shed behind our house. I never got to accumulate much of a flock because of the predatory instincts of our neighbor's cat. I contrived a trap door with an anvil poised to crush said cat but somehow that wily feline managed to budget his nine lives to elude my plot to end his pigeon devouring days.

My favorite days on the farms I visited were the times when the harvest was brought in to be threshed. What fun! That's when I got to drive the hay rack to go out in the field and have the big guys pitch in the grain bundles. When it was full, I'd get to drive the load up to the threshing machine where we would help pitch the bundles into the hungry jaws of the grain separator. We didn't realize how dangerous those machines were . . . but I have since heard some horror stories by my brother of men who fell into the threshing machines and ended up pretty much as mince meat. There is one story of the doctor who was called to the scene, giving the victim a shot from a needle which put him out of his misery. A rather grim story, but reflective of the hard realities of the times.

Another pleasant part of threshing time was the bountiful food. . . tons of fried chicken, sandwiches, cake, lemonade in unlimited supply that we town kids were unaccustomed to. All in all, my experiences on farms as a youngster must have been very healthy besides being a load of fun.

THE RADIO

The 1920's saw the birth of radio due to the genius of Mr. Marconi and other electronic geniuses. Although our home was not among those with the early radios, I was able to have a few "listens" to the early days broadcasts. Somebody in town had a crystal set radio, so I was able to stand in line one afternoon to listen to Aimee Semple McPherson, the California evangelist. You may recall some of her escapades when she was alledgedly kidnapped, but turned out to have been playing house with a boyfriend in the mountains. Aimee was a predecessor of all the T.V. halleluja hucksters who keep begging for money on T.V. today. She was one of the first of her kind and built up a tidy fortune.

But, getting back to radio—the crystal set receiver was a simple device with a tiny piece of galena mineral about the size of a bean. This crystal changed radio waves into audible sounds without the use of batteries or tubes. Since it was quite simple, it was easy to build and many people constructed their own crystal sets with a few yards of wire, an oatmeal box to wind the wire around, and an earphone. Hooking this device up to a long aerial brought in a surprisingly strong signal from far off stations. Tuning was accomplished by a scratch tuner that could be adjusted to touch various parts of the coil.

Developing rapidly at the same time were tube type radios with elaborate tuning devices controlled by one, two, or more knobs on the front panel. It was a feat of skill to bring in a station, adjusting all the knobs until the maximum signal was received. Then,

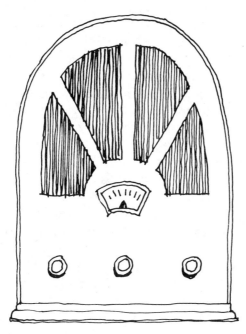

like as not, after a half hour or so, the signal would drift and the tuning would have to commence again. As the number of tubes increased, so did the volume available to be heard. Thus, loud speakers replaced earphones and the family and neighbors could sit around and enjoy this fantastic phenomenon.

Radio became the magic word...coast to coast networks sprang up. Local stations started...some of them experimentally. Some stations faltered and went off the air. Others prospered and became important institutions. The Grand Ole Opry, for example, arose from the weekly broadcasts on WSM in Nashville. WLS in Chicago was owned by Sears, the letters standing for "World's Largest Store."

Usually, a long wire had to be stretched from the house to a point 100 feet away. It seemed the longer the aerial, the better the reception. As for programs, the first I can recall hearing at the local hardware store was JACK ARMSTRONG, ALL AMERICAN BOY. Since we had no radio at home, I got to listen when I wanted to because my playmate's dad was co-owner of the hardware store.

The local restaurant also had a radio and the town folk and country folk would sip coffee and listen to Amos and Andy and a handful of other programming available at that time. There were perhaps 2 or 3 radio stations in South Dakota in 1929, compared to 70 or so at this time.

When we moved to the "big city" in 1935, we finally obtained our first family radio, a handsome cabinet radio called Aetna. It had foreign bands and we could actually bring in London and other far off points. But mainly we gathered around in the evening to hear Edgar Bergen and Charlie McCarthy, Lux Radio Theater, Eddie Cantor, Jack Benny, plus a host of popular shows of the day. Radio stars automatically became movie stars because their names and personalities had become so famous. That is why so many films with Edgar Bergen, Abbott and Costello, Eddie Cantor, Bob Hope and others were made. A radio star. . . in spite of the quality of the film, was almost a guarantee of success at the box office.

Would you believe people used to "watch" their radios? It's true. . . because when the programs were on, everyone listened intently. And since the radio program was being concentrated on so intently, people's eyes tended to focus on the radio set. And with Fibber McGee and Molly, people's imaginations allowed them to mentally "see" the scenario. Radio series lasted longer in those days than most T.V. shows today, possibly because your personal imagination had a lot to do with appeciating the program content. Nowadays, the T.V. show is a real phenomenon if it can last past 13 weeks.

Radio served people in many ways, with news and entertainment, market reports for farmers, and during the depression, Franklin D. Roosevelt's fireside chats helped to maintain the morale of an almost beaten nation. His speeches apparently inspired confidence while the country lifted itself out of the worst depression in history.

MY NORWEGIAN MOTHER

Back in my early childhood. . . when I was three or four
I'd follow Mother 'round the house and tag along to the
    store.
I got to lick the frosting pan and even clean the spoon
And that meant tasty chocolate cake would be appearing
    soon.

I liked to wash the dishes, although my help was meager
But Mother let me "help" her some, because I was so
    eager.
As I grew older I fetched wood to feed the old cook stove.
I even hauled in branches that I picked up in the grove.

Sometimes Mom made lefse. . . it tasted like a dream!
And Krumkake in a cone-shape which she filled up with
    whipped cream
The delicious home-made bread she baked has not been
    equaled since
And Christmas bread with raisins. . . made me feel just like
    a prince.

Although it was depression time, she kept us warmly
    dressed
Her thread and needle skillfully helped her children look
    their best
Even though we were poor in money, in spirit we were
    wealthy
With Mother's care and loving heart, we survived and we
    were healthy.

With "Jesu navn gaar vi til bords" we learned our table
    prayer
She taught respect and honesty and always dealing fair
Yes, Mom was strict. . . but loving; good behavior was a
    must
So we learned reliability, as well as faith and trust.

Mom never made the social world and she wasn't society's
  belle
But people always loved her and often they would tell
Of how she helped out others who had a load to bear
And gave with full and generous heart of what she had to
  share.

At Yuletide, since the times were hard, we made no
  Christmas list
But somehow little presents came. . . so we would not be
  missed.
Perhaps a pair of mittens or a stocking cap of wool
Sometimes a little candy, or taffy we could pull.

By and by our Mom grew old, and infirmities began.
For, raising kids is stressful in a mother's long life span
But she'd sit there in her rocker and dream of fjords so
  deep
And read Decorah Posten 'til she would fall asleep.

She spoke about her mother and her father who'd
  remained
Back in the "gamle land" she loved and never saw again.
The tears would sometimes flow a bit, and mist would fill
  her eyes
Until grandchildren came to call and bring Grandma a
  surprise.
Dear Mother's gone, in heaven now, with rest eternally
I know that God is good to her as she was good to me.
I treasure all the years we had. . . for me there'd be no
  other
And I have memories to enjoy. . . of my Norwegian
  Mother.

-E.C. STANGLAND

MY NORWEGIAN FATHER

Growing up is tougher now . . . than many years ago
The modern dad must work quite hard . . . to make the
   money flow.
When I was growing up, my Dad had time to teach me things
To improvise and make my toys . . . from wires and screws
   and springs.

During the depression, cash was hard to find
We grew up without luxeries, but somehow didn't mind
Pa was always handy with tools and bits of wood
He could take most any broken toy and somehow make it
   good.

The wash machine that Mama used was powered just by
    hand
To get the dirty laundry washed, you worked to beat the band
But Papa hooked a pully up. . . to our ancient Model T
So Mama had the first machine that set the housewife free.

Papa came from Norway when he was twenty eight
Hard work doing farming proved to be his fate.
He finally learned some English and basic business skills
That helped him raise a family and pay the grocery bills.

My Dad was just a plain man. . . with no pretense or show.
He never joined a country club or made a lot of dough
He taught me many humble skills with his well-worn pocket
    knife
As well as other handy things I've used throughout my life.
Papa chewed tobacco and smoked a smelly pipe
He was usually philosophical and seldom had a gripe
But now and then he DID cut loose with some rare
    Norwegian talk
Like when he hit his finger or a wagon team would balk.

Farming was his livelihood, although it wasn't big
He harvested with binders and a steam-powered threshing
    rig.
He often shipped his cattle to Chicago on the train
And used the old farm wagon to haul in all the grain.

My father would look after me. . . when I was just a lad.
And, then one day. . . he passed away. . . and left me
    feeling sad.
Somehow I feel he's watching still. . . for him 'twould be no
    bother
For I still feel the influence of. . . My Norwegian Father.

-E.C. STANGLAND

WHAT NICKNAME DID YOU HAVE?

Very few people go through life without acquiring one or more nicknames. Some of them are descriptive, some are even cruel. Like "Shorty." Short people don't need to be reminded. Fat people are sometimes dubbed "Skinny" and even the very tall are sometimes called "Shorty." Reverse humor, apparently.

In my hometown of Hetland, S.D., everybody had a nickname. That is, the guys mostly. It was not only a custom . . . it was practically a MUST. As a result, there are still people past 80 carrying a nickname that was conferred in childhood.

Reaching back in my memory, I can recall "Zib" Melstad; "Obbie" Melstad; "Tootle" Johnson (a brand of overalls he wore as a lad); Guy "Duck" Dutcher; Velda "Chicken" Weidenkopf (because her last name sounded like "chicken coop"). My brother, Wilbur, was dubbed "Gub," my other brother Orville became "Opal." (I wonder how my mother came up with the combination of Orville and Wilbur? I must say she made the Wright choice.)

In Hetland, if your name was Homer, you became "Hobo." A high hairline earned the nickname "Baldy." I picked up the nickname Einstein because I was always experimenting with electricity and weird chemicals. For the most part, the nicknames were part of the family feeling and a friendly, informal atmosphere of cameraderie. I endorse the practice, although not for the sake of cruelty where physical or mental handicaps or stature are concerned. My personal favorite nickname in my hometown was for a farmer known as "One Horse" Johnson. I suppose it was because he farmed with one horse; but the name had a certain rustic charm about it I find hard to resist.

KEROSENE...GONE, BUT NOT FORGOTTEN

An early day servant we seldom think about anymore is plain old oily kerosene. In my childhood, kerosene lamps were still used frequently even though our homes in town had electricity. I can remember my sisters using the kerosene lamp to heat a curling iron so they could give themselves a fancy hair-do back in the 1920s. I don't recall the names of the hair styles, but I recall hearing about "marcels" and other variations that contributed to the styles of the flapper era. Kerosene was also used for space heaters of the day . . . the most common being the little round heater about the size of a cream can. Since heating was pretty crude then, the little space heater was a Godsend when you got up in the morning and the room was ice cold. Then, there were kerosene stoves for the kitchen with a two gallon jug that you turned upside down in its stove receptacle. Then the jug would glug, glug a few times until the kerosene had reached the cut-off level. The smell of burning kerosene was not necessarily unpleasant and I wouldn't mind catching a whiff of it these days. But, alas, everything is now so electrified that you never get a chance to experience the old time smell of burning kerosene lamps and stoves. The homes of the twneties and thirties even developed a distinctive aroma as they absorbed the kerosene fragrance.

THE SLIDING HILL

Our small town was a typical prairie village, flat as a pool table...with the exception of one hill on the east side. This was our "sliding hill." Winter days would attract dozens of us to walk up the hill and slide down from morning until way past dark. Nobody owned skis, and a lucky few owned a sled. I always had to borrow, since our family couldn't afford a sled. But I managed to scrounge up enough borrowed sleds to get wet to the skin and chilled to the bone every winter day.

To warm up, we went up to the grain elevator nearby where Jerry Bunday tolerantly allowed our gang of kids to warm up around the pot bellied stove. Our further delight was to parch corn on top of the stove. I never forgot Jerry's kindness because I realized later that most businesses don't want kids hanging around, dripping snow all over the floor.

WHEN THE FUNNIES
WERE REALLY FUNNY

My conception of heaven when I was very young. . .was to own an ice cream store and have an unlimited supply of funny papers. Aside from those celestial commodities, I would have no other needs. The funnies were really comic strips. . .and you could become addicted to them much as people get hooked on soap operas today. There was real life drama in "THE GUMPS", "TOOTS AND CASPER", "TILLIE THE TOILER", plus dozens of others. "Bringing up Father" was really Maggie and Jiggs with the legendary Irishman eternally catching heck from the constantly grouchy Maggie, and Jiggs forever heading for Dinty Moore's Tavern, always longing for and consuming his favorite corned beef and cabbage. Andy Gump had a very rich Uncle Bim, a wife name Min, and a little boy, Chester. In Toots and Casper, another family strip there was a rich relative, Uncle Everett. How I longed to have one rich relative because they seemed to always have a solution for family economic problems with their legendary endless source of riches. It seemed that the only relatives we had were of very modest means and those who may have had some money did not acknowledge our existence. I guess times haven't changed. . .poor relations are never popular.

Other favorites were "KATZENJAMMER KIDS", "POPEYE", "DICK TRACY", "BOOB McNUTT", "HAPPY HOOLIGAN", "LITTLE JIMMY", "THE NEBBS", "MAJOR HOOPLE", "BUCK ROGERS", "FLASH GORDON", "BARNEY GOOGLE", "HAROLD TEEN", "LITTLE ORPHAN ANNIE", "WINNIE WINKLE, THE BREADWINNER", "MUTT AND JEFF", "SMILIN JACK", plus dozens of others that now fade into the oblivion of my memory. But at the time, I lived for Monday, which is when the more well-fixed people of our town would discard their Sunday Funnies. (My favorites were in the Chicago Herald and Examiner and the New York Sunday News.) Nowadays, I wouldn't give you a nickel for most of the funny paper sections, loaded with ads and social problems. Bring back Moon Mullins...please!

MAMA AND THE MODEL T

The only cars we ever had were Model-T Fords. The first one I remember was a "touring" model, sort of a convertible. You could drive with the top down, or you could put up the side curtains and have a more-or-less enclosed car. In those days, heaters were unknown, but horse blankets served the purpose nicely.

Anyway, the time came when Mama was forced to take steps to learn how to drive the old Model T Ford. She really didn't want to because she had never learned to drive. But since she had started a dry cleaning shop in Arlington, 5 miles away, it became a daily necessity for her to make the trip. For economy's sake, it was decided that Mama would learn to drive to Arlington, otherwise Papa would have to take her and that would mean two round trips by the end of the day. So, one day, with just the barest of instructions from Papa (half in Norwegian and half in English) Mama stalwartly headed the old Model T out of town on the gravel road. Somehow, a half mile north of town, all of Papa's instructions took flight from her memory, and she was faced with the dilemma of how to slow down the car and turn the corner. Apparently she froze and the tin lizzy rolled into the dead end, went into the ditch and into the farm fence where it mercifully came to a halt.

Later in the day when she had been rescued and calmed, she excitedly explained to Papa in Norwegian the harrowing details of driving that "crasy ting" that she was never going to drive again.

And she didn't. . .that car or ANY car. As Mama said, "Vunce is enough."

THE MEANING OF "UFF DA"

"Uff Da is not in the dictionary, but for many Scandinavians, it is an all-purpose expression covering a variety of situations such as:

Uff Da is . . . looking in the mirror and discovering . . . you're not getting better, you're just getting older.

Uff Da is . . . trying to dance the polka to rock and roll music.

Uff Da is . . . losing your wad of gum in the chicken yard.

Uff Da is . . . eating hot soup when you've got a runny nose.

Uff Da is . . . waking yourself up in church with your own snoring.

Uff Da is . . . sneezing so hard that your false teeth end up in the bread plate.

Uff Da is . . . walking way downtown and then trying to remember what you wanted.

Uff Da is . . . getting swished in the face with a cow's wet tail.

Uff Da is . . . trying to pour two buckets of manure into one bucket.

Uff Da is . . . eating a delicious sandwich and then discovering the spread is cat food.

Uff Da is. . . *arriving late at a lutefisk supper and getting served minced ham instead.*

Uff Da is. . . *when your two "steady" girl friends find out about each other.*

Uff Da is. . . *trying to look at yourself in the mirror January 1st.*

Uff Da is. . . *looking in your rear view mirror and seeing flashing red lights.*

Uff Da is. . . *the same as Charlie Brown's "Good Grief."*

Uff Da is. . . *pushing the light switch and suddenly remembering you forgot to pay the electric bill.*

Uff Da is. . . *opening up the latest real estate tax bill.*

Uff Da is. . . *noticing non-Norwegians at a church dinner using lefse for a napkin.*

Uff Da is. . . *watching what dogs do to lutefisk piled up in front of the butcher shop.*

Uff Da is. . . *not being Scandinavian.*

THE CIRCUS COMES TO TOWN

A small town of 200 residents never attracted much in the way of entertainment. But one summer day, the circus came to town. I had heard stories about kids working their way into the circus by watering the elephants, so I hung around while the tent was being put up—until someone enlisted me as a water carrier.

It was my first circus and the first time I had seen an elephant and probably any other animal outside of a dog, cat or farm critter.

The main object of my fascination was the Fat Lady who was to be exhibited in the side show. I hung around, transfixed, to see a woman so huge. She must have weighed over 500 pounds. Even though I was only about 9 years old, I can still hear the fat lady, who had noticed me staring, as she testily ordered me, "Don't gawk!" To this day, whenever I see an overly corpulent woman, the words pop into my mind, "Don't gawk."

CARS, CARS AND MORE CARS

In the twenties and thirties, the automobile scene was a whole different story compared to today. For one thing, there were no Japanese or German compacts and sub-compacts tooling around. But there was plenty of chrome and fancy car bodies as America's love affair with the automobile evolved. Large wheels were a "must" to get through mudholes on the road. A jack was standard equipment, but not the bumper jack that we know today. It was usually a crank type, very clumsy, that you got down on your hands and knees to shimmy under the rear axle. Then, crank like heck to get that heavy body up in the air; careful though. . .put a block under one wheel so that car didn't roll off the jack. Fixing a tire was often a killer, due largely to the difficult task of removing the tire from the rim; I can recall sweating and cussing over jimmying a tire off the rim of a '28 Oldsmobile I bought after the war (WW II, that is.)

The variety of cars was magnificent. Do you recall any of these names? Rockne; Whippet; Hudson; Terraplane; Essex; Rickenbacker (a little before MY time); Overland; La Salle; De Soto; LaFayette; Franklin; Nash; Star; Studebaker; Model T and Model A Fords; Cord; Reo; Oakland. Later on came the short-lived Kaiser, Fraser, and Tucker. (Not to forget the Henry J.) A trip through a car museum such as Harrah's in Reno can give you a real shot of nostalgia for the old time flivvers and limousines that are part of America's automotive heritage. It has been a long trip since people in buggies shouted at auto drivers, "Get a horse!"

chari va ri (Fr.) a mock serenade of discordant noises made on kettles, tin horns, etc.; often played as a practical joke on newly married couples: Also "shivaree."

A "Chivari" was a small town custom whereby the people would come to the home of a newly married couple and rouse them out by making a racket with kettles or bells. The object was to have the couple come out and be transported up town in a lumber wagon or other crude conveyance. There, the newlyweds, by tradition, were expected to "treat" the crowd with pop and candy bars. The newlyweds as a rule put up with it, first of all to stop the racket outside their window, and because it was expected of them. They would try to accept the Chivari good naturedly, hoping that the financial tab would not be over-burdening, even at a nickel a candy bar and a nickel for pop. Sometimes the men in the crowd would get cigars; the kids came along to kibitz and get any treats forthcoming. The newlyweds did not ordinarily go on a honeymoon, so a Chivari was probably secretly enjoyed as part of the small community recognition of the marriage.

"MOTHER'S ROCKING CHAIR"

*In a lifetime full of memories, there is one we
all can share
The memory of a mother, gently rocking in a chair
My recollections call to mind. . . from early
childhood years
The countless hours my mother rocked in happiness
and tears.*

The tragedies of childhood, the everyday mishap
Most any ache or fever would subside there in her lap
No matter what the ailment, her rocking did the trick
It was her standard treatment when any child was sick.

When times were hard and food was scarce. . .
    and money mighty rare
We'd often see our mother, rocking in her chair
By and by solutions to our problem came to mind
As mother thought out ways and means to ease
    financial bind.

As we grew up and went on dates, I clearly can recall
The sound of Mother rocking as I tiptoed in the hall.
She'd been there rocking many hours, as near
    as I could tell
Then silently she went to bed, assured that all was well.

My brother and I went off to war and crossed
    the ocean foam.
Many foreign lands we saw before we got back home.
As I came walking to our house, in the window
    I saw there
The figure of my mother, rocking in her chair.

As Mom grew old and illness came, with shawl
    upon her lap
I often found her resting, rocking 'til she'd nap
It somehow eased her many pains and passed
    the time away
Until her children came to call, to visit or to stay.

Grandchildren were her special joy. . . and while the tots
    were small
Mom would proudly rock them and quiet every squall
No one could soothe the children like Grandma
    in her chair
For it was her special duty to pacify them there.

One day her chair fell silent. . . as it stood there
    on the floor
For Mom had gone to heaven. . . to rest forevermore
Hopefully we'll meet again in a reunion there
And I expect to see my Mother, sitting,
    rocking in her chair.

-E.C. STANGLAND

LIVING THROUGH THE DEPRESSION

Mention the word "depression" nowadays and people will think you are talking about a mental condition where you go to a psychiatrist and talk to him for an hour while he prepares a bill for you to pay him $80. During the REAL depression, back in the late 20's and all of the 30's, that $80 would have kept a family well fed for two or three months. Yes, I'm talking HARD TIMES, the DIRTY THIRTIES. After the crash of '29, former millionaires jumped out of windows and once-prosperous people went begging in the streets. In our small town, we felt the impact all right, but I doubt that it was devastating as in the larger cities. My family was already used to hard times by 1929, my dad having lost everything he had to a crooked banker in 1925.

In recent times, I have seen people walk out of grocery stores with big thick T-bone steaks bought with food stamps. During the depression of the 30's, even hamburger was considered a luxury. The main way we survived was by knowing how to do without. Luxuries were not difficult to forego; clothing was a bit tougher, but by wearing things out and patching what was left, and wearing hand-me-downs, we were able to get by. Food was one of the hardest things to cut down on because people simply have to eat. It was just a matter of making things stretch...having home baked bread, homemade soap, eating the simple foods that didn't cost much. I'm here to tell you that I was practically brought up on oatmeal, and surprisingly, I still like it. Sour cream and homemade bread was another favorite, especially when sprinkled with sugar. We raised our own poultry, kept a cow in our backyard, and squeaked by with a little help from the relief agency when things got really tough.

Those were the days, around 1934, when WPA saved the day for numerous families. There simply was no other form of income for many people. Some folks who were fortunate enough to have a means of support sneered at WPA workers, accusing them of leaning on shovels all day. Millions of young men, including my two brothers, went to CCC camps where they did useful work to improve state properties while earning a modest amount of money to send home. Believe me, going through the depression is a hard lesson in living, but guaranteed to make you appreciate good times and have a feeling for those who are down on their luck. I never want to go through it again, but I don't regret the experience.

RUN SHEEP RUN

Our favorite childhood pastime usually involved a
bunch of kids and one of the many games we played:
Run Sheep, Run; Annie I Over; I Send; Hide and Go
Seek; Ole, Ole, Outs in Free . . . just a few examples of
games I can no longer remember how to play. Well,
maybe I could still muster up a game of hide and go
seek, but being Norwegian, who would want to find
me? Then there was Mumblety Peg, played with a jack

knife where you tried to flip the knife to land in various positions to win a game. And Tiddley Winks, flipping small disks into a cup; Marbles, of course, was a universal childhood favorite. . . draw a line in the dirt and see who could come closest. We could buy clay marbles like 10 for a penny. Agates, glassies and steelies cost more.

Somehow, we never ran out of things to do, games to play, innocent childhood pursuits to keep our minds and bodies active. From swinging in a tire swing to having fun on a teeter totter, childhood was a blissful time of no responsibility and carefree days and nights.

We were unaware of the problems that grownups had, even our parents. There were grasshoppers to be caught and kept in a jar, mud to be played with, water to throw at each other, and games to play day after lazy day. Run Sheep Run and the other games were exciting to us youngsters and it would do my heart good to see a gang of kids playing such games today. Seems to me kids grow up too fast nowadays and are too much aware of the problems of the world. Small wonder so many of them turn to drugs and alcohol to escape.

How many memories do YOU share? A hand pump in the kitchen with a simple sink, a pail under it to catch the water, or a pipe leading to the outside of the house where it fell on the ground; washing your hands and face in a porcelain coated metal wash basin. If the pump got dried out and wouldn't deliver water, why, all you had to do was pour some in from the water dipper and prime the pump by pumping the handle a few times. Lord, wouldn't it be fun to prime a pump again? Wouldn't it feel good to wash your face in an old fashioned wash basin again with a bar of Castile soap to take off the grime. Wouldn't it smell good to have an old fashioned cook stove all fired up in an old fashioned kitchen, ready to bake up a batch of old fashioned baked bread? My mother made the best homemade bread in the world, and her raisin bread was a special delicacy, flavored subtly with cardamom seed and the crust glazed lightly with sugar water. I challenge modern bakeries to come out with a product as good as Mom baked right at home.

WASH DAY

For washing clothes for seven people, Mama would use the old wash tub and the copper boiler, plus the old wooden washing machine we acquired about 1925. Even though I was only 3, I can recall the machine with its hand propelled dasher mechanism. You made the washer work by grabbing the handle and moving it back and forth. To say the least, this was strenuous work. But, Papa being of an inventive bent, figured out a way to mechanize wash day with a power supply close at hand. We owned a Model T Ford, so Pa came up with a home-made wooden pulley about the size of a king size birthday cake. This pulley would then be bolted to the rear right wheel of the Model T, and Pa would run a belt to the pulley of the washing machine by putting a jack under the rear axle, the right rear wheel would spin by itself without moving the car, thus powering the washing machine without human labor. It was amazing to the neighbors who hadn't yet acquired a motorized washing machine. The wringer, of course, still had to be worked manually with a crank.

Washing in the winter was a tougher job. . .I can recall the long underwear hanging on the line where they became frozen like mannequins in the icy temperatures. Then they would be brought in the house and hung over a wooden clothes drying rack placed over the furnace grate. Until we moved to the

Big Town when I was 13, I never remember a winter when we didn't have clothes drying out between the living room and dining room. Another wash day appurtenance I forgot to mention is the old fashioned Wash Board. . .essential in every home. How long has it been since you've seen an honest to goodness wash board? Mama used to rub her knuckles raw trying to get the dirt out of clothes for seven people. And with hard water and home-made soap. How about that, you housewives of today? Still think you are over worked with your electric dishwasher, microwave oven, deep freeze, automatic washer and dryer?

WELL, THAT'S SHOE BIZ

You don't know what hard times are all about if you have never had to cut out cardboard to put in your shoes after the sole had worn through. They were not completely weather proof, but the cardboard make-do was the best some of us could manage when there weren't enough dollars to supply each kid with new shoes when childhood play activity had worn them through all too quickly. Back in the thirties there was a kit you could buy consisting of a glue-on rubber sole and a little tube of glue. So, many was the time that, in place of cardboard, I would glue a rubber sole on the bottom of one or more of my shoes. These soles would work fine...at least for a little while. But unfortunately, the cement was not always dependable and part of the rubber sole would work loose. So, there you'd be, on the way to school, with a rubber sole flapping every step you took. How embarrassing, for it sounded to the wearer just like a thunder clap, telling everyone around you, you had to wear a rubber sole because you couldn't afford a new pair of shoes. If by chance you could have the shoes half-soled by the local shoemaker, that worthy gentleman would use short nails to affix a new leather sole. Somehow, the nails were not always flattened down properly and a sharp nail would start working into your foot with every step. So, we depression kids were frequently seen with a temporary limp until we could settle down long enough to find a hammer to flatten the pesky nail or nails. It seems hard to realize now that the common necessities today are so easy to obtain, but in the depression days, if you came from a poor family every item of clothing meant taking away the family food supply.

THE PARTY LINE

Our family finally managed to have a telephone...a wall model with a crank to call "Central." Everyone was on a party line and your individual ring would be like a Morse Code. Two longs and three shorts, for example. And if you happened to lift the receiver and listen to someone else's conversation, that was known as "rubbering." But, it proved to be the most effective news medium of the era with no secrets kept when mentioned on the party line telephone. The operator, I suspect, had excellent access to local gossip not available to today's computerized and recorded telephone operators.

"WHITE HANDKERCHIEFS"
(On a departure from Norway)

In Eighteen Eighty One, my Uncle Gudmund left his land
His home in southern Norway where the noble
   mountains stand
The fjords and emerald pastures were part of
   Nordic scenes
Where Uncle was a shepherd boy of humble
   worldly means.

His dreams were of America where fortune he would find
Ambitious youth inspired him to leave his home behind
And so one day he left them, the folks he loved so well;
For America was calling, and he was in its spell.

He took his meager luggage to the dock where he'd depart
But leaving all his loved ones. . . nearly broke his heart
And as the boat moved slowly from the shore
   out to the bay
He was seeing his last glimpses of his native land,
   Norway.

He looked intently toward the shore. . . the picture
   was preserved
To etch into his memory the sights that he observed
The last thing he remembered, as he would later tell,
Was the sight of those white handkerchiefs that waved
   a last farewell.

White handkerchiefs...they fluttered...a signal
  of goodbye
More poignant than the spoken word, more stirring
  than a cry.
The tears came freely then as Uncle Gudmund gripped
  the rail
His handkerchief he waved to them, and it fluttered
  like a sail.

White handkerchiefs. . . white handkerchiefs. . .
  remembered evermore
The final sight of loved ones as he left dear Norway's shore
America's promise beckoned and a new life
  waited there. . .
In time, a wife and family and a farm for all to share.

But Uncle Gudmund ne'er forgot events that passed before
The memory of white handkerchiefs, waving
  from the shore
White handkerchiefs. . . white handkerchiefs. . .
  they help me understand
How painful was departure from my Uncle's native land.

-E.C. STANGLAND

ROLLING TIRES AND HOOPS

If I ever see a youngster roll a tire down the street, I am going to stand transfixed for a good half hour with my jaw agape. We rolled a lot of tires back in the twenties and thirties. Why? Because it gave us something to do. Because it was free. Because it was fun. Just get a discarded tire and start rolling. Up one street, down the next. No batteries required. . .just kid-energy.

Same goes for rolling a hoop. This, however, necessitated a lath with a cross stick at the end. Grab the lath on the end, hook the cross stick in the hoop and start rolling. We learned some fancy tricks, too, putting fancy spins on the hoop, hopping curbs, and spending hours just rolling that darn hoop all over town.

Don't ask me why it was so much fun. . .I just remember that it WAS. Maybe what this world needs is more tire rolling, hoop rolling and less valium. (You ought to try it sometime. . .when nobody is watching, of course. See what it does for your tensions.)

THE POPCORN WAGON & MOVIES

Recently, my wife and I went to a movie which cost us $8. One helping of popcorn and one cup of soda pop cost us $2. Total bill: $10. Talk about inflation! Compare that to the times when a movie cost anywhere from a nickel to a quarter and popcorn rarely over 5¢. That must represent at least 3,000% inflation.

Movies in the 20's and 30's had NO swearing in them, no dirty words. And yet, they were EXCITING. Theaters were packed. But, of course, that was before people became jaded and had to have shootings, killings, violence of all kinds to induce them to sit and watch a movie for a couple of hours.

For some reason, the early movies didn't sell popcorn to its customers. . . at least in our locality. That was usually the job for the local popcorn wagon operator. Nearly every town had one. Even though Hetland didn't have a regular full time movie house, we did have a small popcorn wagon. The larger towns had the now-classical popcorn wagon that you could smell for blocks, the tantalizing aroma luring you like a narcotic. You still see one now and then, such as in the Chicago airport. . . a little link with the past but somehow never the same as when they were a regular part of the street scene all over the U.S. of A.

RUG BEATING

Up until the late 30's, I was still a reluctant volunteer for rug beating. Of all the ignominious chores my mother could think up for me to do, that was about the worst. We didn't have a vacuum cleaner for a long time, so the standard procedure in getting some of the dirt out of the rugs was to roll them up and take them outdoors to sling over a couple of clothes lines for a good rug beating. Remember the old rug beater? A twisted wire affair with a handle on the end which you would grip and whale the tar out of the rugs. When Mama began remarking that the rugs were getting dirty, I would try to arrange a quick escape before she could grab my collar and mention (polite word for DEMAND) that I should get busy beating the rugs. Oh well, I thought, win a few, lose a few. Most times I lost because Mama could out-think me.

THE HOOSE GOW

Hetland's tiny jail was a small one-person cage located within the walls of the town pump house. The only people I saw in jail were occasional drunks and a vagrant or two. No pistol packing cops, no handcuffs. Just a little cage to cool off whoever needed cooling off. Perhaps that is why a jail is sometimes called a "cooler."

BOXCAR WILLIES OF
THE DEPRESSION

When the depression hit in 1929, a common daily sight was the boxcars going through Hetland festooned with dozens of non-paying riders. We called them hoboes, and I guess that is what they were. But basically, they were part of the enormous army of unemployed who were victims of the great depression. I was too young to understand the significance of this phenomenon, but I could see my mother's reaction as she tearfully watched the mournful sight of homeless men, riding the boxcars to Lord knows where. It was depressing even for a child and I hope we never have to see it again.

KIDS SMOKING

Back in the 20s and 30s, smoking was considered the ultimate in masculinity and maturity. Kids could hardly wait to get started on the weed. Tobacco was considered a family necessity (for papa) right along with food and clothing. The more conservative men, for the sake of thrift perhaps, chose a pipe. Smoking tobacco was usually Prince Albert, Sir Walter Raleigh, Model, or Velvet. (A typical kid gag in those days was to call the local general store merchant and ask "Do you have Prince Albert in the can?" If an affirmative answer was given, the punch line came: "WELL, LET HIM OUT." Then giggles, and hang up the receiver on the phone hook which disconnected the conversation.) But, back to tobacco. The aforementioned brands were the most popular, but a few, like my Dad, who liked more bite in their tobacco, chose a stronger brand in a large tin foil pouch, such as Adams Standard. Snoose chewing was also a regular habit with many and spitting was commonplace. . . in spittoons in public places, on the streets, or in one-gallon tin cans for those who chose not to invest in a brass spittoon.

Small wonder that we kids longed to become smokers. My companions chose not to experiment with real tobacco, but corn silk was considered just the ticket to get started on. Since cigarette paper was not generally available to kids, newspapers were torn to make homemade corn silk cigarettes. Naturally, an out of the way place had to be found, for experimental smoking was very much frowned upon. I had the urge to try corn silk (which was, by the way, not inhaled) and then one day someone pointed out that the "big kids" smoked string as well. So, we had to try out smoking string. And, what a noxious experience! But feeling we had to try it out, we chose Bud Knudsen's backyard where 3 of us lit up with farmer matches and tried to find out what was so great about string smoking. We quickly learned that the main thrill was that of doing something covert and forbidden. And then, to our mortification we were caught by Bud's folks. We scattered. I knew there would be hell to pay because I was sure Bud's mother would tell my Mom. So, I opted for going into hiding. I couldn't imagine what punishment would be forthcoming, but I dreaded the unknown penalty. . . maybe thinking that time would be on my side, therefore staying underground until hopefully the storm might blow over. At first, I hid with my two co-conspirators in a grain elevator cubby hole. After a half hour, the other kids chickened out and ran home. I joined them, but instead of surrendering, I climbed in the bedroom window of my house and hid in the closet, well protected behind my Mother's dresses. Soon I could hear voices speculating as my whereabouts. As dusk fell, anxiety filled Mother's voice. Finally, I heard Mom say, "Well, if he don't show up by six o'clock, we better have them blow da fire whistle." (Hetland had a fire whistle that doubled as a six o'clock supper time signal each night. Also, it could be used for emergencies to summon the community for a dire situation. . .such as a missing kid who had been smoking string.) Well, that did it, and out I came from my closet hibernation. My Mother's reaction was mixed with relief and a conviction that I must be punished. So, she ordered me to go outside and gather some birch branches for a switch so that I might receive a deserved "licking." Needless to say, I came back with the flimsiest, rottenest twigs I could find. And somehow I noted that Mom's administration of the "switch" was half hearted, mixed as it was with relief for my emerging safe and sound. This was my first and last experiment with string, as well as corn silk!

UNCLE TORVALD'S
CHRISTMAS CAROL

T'vas da night before Christmas and each little Norsk
Vas dreaming of rommegrot, lefse and torsk
Our stockings had holes and dey hung by da door
Dere vasn't no fireplace because ve vas poor.

Da times had been hard and Pa vas laid off
Grandpa vas sick and he had a bad cough
Sister and brudder vere needing new shoes
And Mama vas feeling da "No money" blues.

Along about midnight ven ve vere in bed
I heard a big racket out dere by da shed
And den as I listened, I heard loud and clear
"ON Axel! ON Torger! Let's get out of here."

Next morning I voke and to da vindow I crept
And dere vas a sack laying on da back step
It vas yammed full of presents. . .Oh! Vhat a trill!
And for each vun of us. . .a ten dollar bill!

Oh, dat vas da merriest Christmas of all
I can still hear Santa's Christmas eve call:
"ON Axel! ON Torger! Let's get out of here!"
I vas sure it vas Santa. . .it sounded so clear.

Yet, somehow dat voice seemed familiar to me
And I noticed big hoofprints out by da oak tree
Den I remembered Mr. Knutson who lived across town
Who always helped others ven deir luck vas down.

Mr. Knutson had horses and he owned a big sled
I thought it all over dat night in my bed
"God bless Santa," I said. Then, with a grin,
"And God bless Mr. Knutson, 'cause I tink it vas him."

-E.C. STANGLAND

MY KINGDOM FOR A HORSE

As a youngster, one of the great thrills was to be privileged to drive a team and wagon. I would volunteer any time just to have the experience of holding the reins, call out "giddap" and have the fun of driving a team. Mostly my experiences were with Babe and Nellie, Ole Peterson's dray horses. Ole was pretty lenient with kids.

Other times, I would drive teams of horses at nearby farms where a bit of volunteer work was often welcome. I think the biggest share of the thrill of driving a team of horses was that of having a vehicle under my control . . . very similar to the grown up feeling when you started learning to drive a car. We never owned a horse while I was growing up, nor have I ever had an urge to own one in adult life. But for a kid in the 20's and 30's, it was a pretty special experience to hold on to the reins, and with a high pitched "giddap" get that powerful team to move a load of oats or a hayrack full of bundles across a farmstead.

BOX SOCIALS

A box social was a custom in our town to raise money for school activities. Each of the girls would put together a box of goodies, such as sandwiches, cake or cookies. Then, at the Box Social, the public would gather at the school house and bid on the fance wrapped boxes filled with food. The idea was that whoever bid the highest on a box at the social would have the privilege of sharing it with the girl who made it. This was a form of courting, I suppose, because the favorite girls would see their lunches bid up sky high prices, sometimes as much as $2.50; and the high bidder then would triumphantly enjoy the company of his favorite, all the better to get acquainted. It is not known how many marriages culminated from this custom, but it was very popular because it gave the guys a chance to express their admiration in a socially acceptable way.

MORE CHILDHOOD MEMORIES

You are a child of the twenties if you can remember spending a lot of time delving in junk yards for some salvageable treasure. Did you ever make a rubber gun out of a board from the end of a peach or orange crate and some 3/4 inch rubber bands cut from an old inner tube? Did you ever get a black eye like I did from catching a rubber gun projectile at close range?

Can you remember when everyone in town had outhouses, and the height of luxury was when canning season came around, you got to use the soft wrappers from fresh peaches? Do you recall OIL CLOTH and LINOLEUM floor covering? (Gosh, maybe they still make linoleum. I haven't seen a roll of it in years.)

As a kid, did you ever make a "telephone" out of two tin cans and a length of string? They worked, too...a little.

Were you a kid that sold seeds or snaps door to door, hoping to win some premiums from a catalog? Or maybe you sold Cloverine salve with the prospect of earning a guitar. Do you recall spending hours in abandoned cars in someone's back yard, making noises like a car, pretending you were driving? How about...depression glass in pink, yellow and green...which is worth a fortune today?

If you remember these, welcome to the club of Old Timers. For better or worse, THOSE were the good old days although we all enjoy the modern conveniences. (Excuse me, I have to go check my VCR and make sure I get a tape of the Star Trek re-run.)

JUNK COLLECTING

If you were a kid in a small town like Hetland, you had to become skilled in scrounging up money for your necessities, like candy, ice cream and firecrackers. One money source was selling old brass and copper to the junkman who came in from Lake Preston every so often. We kids knew where all the dumping grounds were, so we made periodic trips to unearth discarded metal items like copper boilers, brass nozzles and other nonferrous metals. We soon became expert in determining whether a metal was brass or copper by using an old magnet from a discarded crank telephone. What didn't stick to the magnet, we would haul into town to sell to the junkman. With a little luck and perseverence, we could sometimes net 25 to 50 cents from our junk forays. We would never take property still in use, or steal any properly owned items... our morality was impeccable due to our home training and the Congregational church.

THE TOWN DRUNKS

In a small town when I was a boy, there were two affinities that youngsters developed early on. One was for dogs, and the other was for the town drunks. Sound strange? I mean, about the drunks? Well, it is simple. The cameraderie between inebriates and kids was based somewhat on their mutual tolerance for each other. Let me explain. The town sot knew his reputation was shot, that everyone looked down on h i m . . .

except kids. Youngsters somehow had a tolerance for wayward individuals. Kids are a lot like dogs that way. They accept you no matter what, as long as you are not a threat to them. So, when we kids would be "hanging around" uptown, and it was early Saturday night, we learned to be on the lookout for the town and country inebriates. They were always in the mood for some jollity, some kidding. And the chances were always good we could run errands for them, such as run over to the drug store for a bottle of pop (their mix with the hard stuff) or a sack of Bull Durham. Such a trip would invariably earn a nickel or a dime . . . sometimes even a quarter. And like as not, we'd get a coin or two just for the heck of it. No such luck from the sober citizens . . . they were always busy going about their business and usually had scant time to josh the youngsters. So, we learned early to congregate where the drinking crowd would gather in town. . . this was during prohibition. . . and there was usually a bottle of booze hidden in the tool box of their Model T Ford.

Sunday morning would find us out north of town where the drinkers had gone to do their heavier drinking the night before. . . discarding the pop bottles when they were done. So, with a gunny sack, we would do pop bottle hunting, invariably yielding a harvest of a dime or more when we turned the bottles in at the drug store. The liquor bottles we left alone because we couldn't sell them. So that explains why kids and drunks got along so well. . . the drunks were so jolly and generous.

PRANKS GROWNUPS PLAYED

A favorite pastime in our town was the practical jokes played on kids. When you reached a certain age, say around 9 or 10, and you were hanging around the barbershop or the drug store, someone would feel impelled to initiate you into the rite of running on a fool's errand. A kid who had learned the potential profit in running errands was an easy mark. "Kid, run over to Nel Nelson's garage and get me a sky hook." Well, I didn't know any better, so I'd run across the street to Nels' garage and tell him Obbie Melstad needed a sky hook. Nels got a funny grin on his face and announced, "I just lent that to Mory Anderson down at the Blacksmith Shop. . . run down there and ask for it." Of course, I bit on the whole scenario, and it took several futile runs around town to realize I'd been had!

Other such pranks involved doughnut stretchers, and left-handed monkey wrenches. Trusting lad that I was, it took me a couple of these experiences before I was to learn that grownups could and would pull a prank on a kid. Outside of learning about Santa Claus, it was my first loss of illusion in what was otherwise a trustworthy world. Others in our town (not me) got taken in by the infamous snipe hunts where the sucker was fooled into holding a sack at the bottom of the hill while the perpetrator was allegedly busy rounding up "snipes."

LOOK AT THE BIRDIE!

Taking snapshots back in the twenties and thirties, was a fairly uncomplicated project, although not devoid of pitfalls. Basically, you were working with a box camera, most likely a Kodak Brownie. They were fairly fool-proof so that any fool could take a picture and have it turn out. Thanks to the simplicity of those box cameras, we now have snapshots to show what life was like in those "good old days."

Since simple flash equipment was not available to the general public, the only indoor shots that we see today were generally the result of time exposures. This necessitated the subjects of the picture to stand as perfectly still as possible and wait while the person taking the picture would count "One thousand, two thousand, three thousand, four thousand," thus timing about 4 seconds. With fairly decent surrounding light, 4 or 5 seconds could give you a decent picture inside a building. You would insert a roll of film purchased at the drug store and then watch the numbers appear through a little red window on the back of the box camera, as you turned the knob. From time to time, someone would forget to wind the film after a snapshot, thus resulting in a double exposure. I have a collection of double exposures saved for some strange reason because there were some recognizable people in the scenes. I often wish that people would have written something on the back of the pictures so that now, 50 years later, we might be able to identify the people in the snaps. I am still trying to figure out

what my half-brother, Hans, looked like, because he died many years ago and his snapshot picture is mixed in with hordes of unidentified relatives, friends and assorted strangers.

THE MOVIES

Movies in our small town were mostly silent. In view of the limited available audience, "moom pitchers" were a once-a-week occasion with a local entrepreneur doing the honors as projectionist, ticket seller and bouncer. A bunch of kids on Saturday could get pretty excited over a western action two-reeler. I can recall just how stimulated a gang of pre-teenage boys could get when the villain would lie in wait for the hero somewhere in western Montana. When it appeared the hero was going to ride into the trap, the excited kids would yell in a chorus: "Don't go! He's got a gun!"

On summer nights, the merchants would frequently chip in and give a free show outside with a bed sheet stretched over Herb Johnson's barn to serve as a screen. Between reels, colorful slides promoting local businesses would be shown. How I'd like to have a collection of those slides today as collectors items!

Going into the thirties—I occasionally got to see "talkies" in neighboring Lake Preston. If the action got too exciting, I would cover up my eyes until more peaceful conditions prevailed. That may give you an idea of the lack of sophistication of our era . . . especially mine.

OLE SAYS...YOU KNOW YOU'RE GETTING OLD WHEN...

Everything hurts and what doesn't hurt, doesn't work.

The gleam in your eyes is from the sun hitting your bifocals.

You feel like the night after, and you haven't been anywhere.

Your little black book contains only names ending in M.D.

You get winded playing chess.

Your children begin to look middle aged.

You're still chasing women but can't remember why.

A dripping faucet causes an uncontrollable bladder urge.

You know all the answers, but nobody asks you the questions.

You look forward to a dull evening.

You walk with your head high trying to get used to your bifocals.

Your favorite part of the newspaper is 25 years ago today.

You turn out the light for economic rather than romantic reasons.

You sit in a rocking chair and can't get it going.

Your knees buckle and your belt won't.

You regret all those mistakes resisting temptation.

You're 17 around the neck, 42 around the waist, and 96 around the golf course.

After painting the town red, you have to take a long rest before applying a second coat.

Dialing long distance wears you out.

You're startled the first time you are addressed as an old timer.

You remember today that your wedding anniversary was yesterday.

You can't stand people who are intolerant.

The best part of your day is over when your alarm clock goes off.

You burn the midnight oil until 9 P.M.

Your back goes out more often than you do.

A fortune teller offers to read your face.

Your pacemaker makes the garage door go up when you watch a pretty girl go by.

The little gray-haired lady you help across the street is your wife.

You get your exercise acting as a pallbearer for your friends who exercise.

You have too much room in the house and not enough room in the medicine cabinet.

THE TOWN PUMP

It was common in the 1920s to see a town pump in most small towns. Ours was no exception. The motorized age was not fully upon us, so a certain amount of horsepower was needed to do all the hauling on the farm and in the villages. So, the town pump was a congregating spot where farmers and townspeople could draw off what water supplies they needed. Eventually, a faucet was installed, but prior to that momentous event, I was to learn one of the basic lessons of life: never try to lick the frost from a frozen pump handle (or door knob). In case you never tried it, I'll explain what happens. Simply, your tongue is immediately frozen to the iron pump handle as surely as though you were stuck by Super Glue. Since I was probably only about 8 or 9 at the time, I don't have a clear recollection of how I got loose. But it was a lesson that has lasted a lifetime that usually doesn't have to be repeated.

THE WOOD PILE

Long before bottle gas, natural gas pipelines, electric heat, fuel oil and the like, there was the Wood Pile age. Everyone in our town had a wood pile so that meant everyone had an axe and a chopping block. Ours was a cottonwood stump that we used to split large wood chunks into kindling wood. Mama used the smaller pieces for her cook stove, while Pa took the heftier pieces for the furnace, which was a dandy supplement for the expensive (to us) coal. I can remember as a boy of 10 being expected to take my turn at the wood chopping chore. And, on several occasions, I had to use the stump as an executioner's block for a chicken to be served for Sunday dinner. I didn't care for that chore much, especially since I befriended some of the chickens as pets and was also somewhat fascinated and horrified at the same time at the sight of a chicken running around our yard minus its head.

In the event you cannot find this book in your town:

REORDER FORM FOR
"O LUTEFISK" (The Book)

NAME _____

ADDRESS _____

CITY, STATE, ZIP _____

No. of Copies _____@ **$6^{95} per copy**

      TOTAL_____**Postage Paid**

Send cash, check or mail order for $6.95 to:
Norse Press, Box 1554, Sioux Falls, S.D. 57101

In the event you cannot find this book in your town:

REORDER FORM FOR
"O LUTEFISK" (The Book)

NAME _____

ADDRESS _____

CITY, STATE, ZIP _____

No. of Copies _____@ **$6^{95} per copy**

      TOTAL_____**Postage Paid**

Send cash, check or mail order for $6.95 to:
Norse Press, Box 1554, Sioux Falls, S.D. 57101